P9-DCR-956

COUNTRY
Decorating

COUNTRY
Decorating

STEWART AND SALLY WALTON

Photographs by James Duncan

SMITHMARK

This edition published in 1996 by
SMITHMARK Publishers
a division of U.S. Media Holdings, Inc.,
16 East 32nd Street
New York, NY 10016

SMITHMARK Books are available for bulk purchase, for sales promotion
and for premium use. For details, write or call the manager of special sales,
SMITHMARK Publishers, 16 East 32nd Street,
New York, NY 10016; (212) 532-6600.

10 9 8 7 6 5 4 3 2

ISBN 0-8317-3611-9

Publisher: Joanna Lorenz
Project editor: Sarah Ainley
Designer: Janet James
Photographer: James Duncan
Stylist: Tessa Evelegh
Illustrator: Nadine Wickenden

Photographs on pp 6–7, 14, 15, 36, 37, 56 and 57 by Steve Tanner.
Photographs on pp 76–87 by Michelle Garrett.
Projects on pp 76–87 by Tessa Evelegh.

Previously published as part of a larger compendium, *Glorious Country*.

Printed In Singapore by Star Standard Industries Pte. Ltd.

Contents

Country Style

Country style has many interpretations, and all over the world there are townspeople who dream of a calmer way of life where life is still governed by seasonal changes and not man-made deadlines. Country homes are alive and growing; country decorating is for living in, not just for looking at. The details may vary with nationality and climate, but the effect remains home-made and functional, comfortable and relaxed. ❧ Country kitchens can be a riot of pattern and colour, where the dresser is stacked with displays of china and the beams are hung with baskets of drying flowers and herbs. Gleaming copper pots and pans are never hidden away in cupboards, but displayed up high on butcher's hooks. Floors need to be practical, tough and easy to clean: floorboards, flagstones, linoleum or cork tiles are the favourite choices, softened with washable cotton dhurries or rag-rugs. Throughout the home, flower arrangements take their cue from nature and are combined with other organic materials to provide a casual, spontaneous look. The country house is not a fashion statement, and its colour scheme should reflect the natural colours in the landscape; these need not be dull or bland; they can be as rich as autumn or as brilliant or as warm as summer. The house responds to personal touches; make time in your life to be creative. ❧ This book shows you how to get into that way of thinking, and how to bring some of the dream of country living into your home. There are step-by-step projects here to suit all levels of experience and creative ability. You may feel daunted by embroidery but more confident about making patterns in tin with a hammer and nail; unsure about flower arranging, but able to pop a few dried flowerheads into a terracotta pot. ❧ Whatever you choose, rest assured that all the projects have been designed to give maximum effect for minimum effort. If you want to ring the changes very quickly on your walls, use a colour glaze with a foamblock print or stencilled

BELOW: The beautiful yet practical nature of patchwork is typical of country style.

border. Giving floorboards the limed look requires the hard work of sanding first, but the painting can be done and dried in an afternoon. If you have considered laying cork tiles, then stain half of them black and make a real impact with a chequer-board floor. When it comes to choosing materials, or pieces of furniture to decorate, take a tip from the squirrel and start hoarding! There are so many second-hand stores, car boot sales and jumble sales around, and if you buy things that have potential, you will always have something to hand when the creative mood strikes. ❧ On a very practical note, there has been a major change in materials for home-decorating recently, with the arrival of water-based paint products. There is no longer any need for

solvents to clean brushes; they rinse out under the tap. The biggest bonus of this revolution is that decorating time has been cut in half. Water-based products dry very quickly, and this is especially useful when apply-ing many coats of varnish to painted furniture. The rule to remember is not to mix oil and water, so if you tint varnish for an antique effect, mix acrylics with water-based clear varnish or oil colour with traditional varnish. ❧ Whether you go for

ABOVE: *Although several motifs are present in this room, the restricted use of colour pulls the whole look together.*

the country look for your home, or just a few details, always try to decorate in a way that is sympathetic to the character and age of your house. Use the best features, like an interesting shaped window, as focal points; be courageous about removing a ghastly fireplace, or disguising oppressively heavy beams. Your home should please you, and country style is about personal touches, natural materials, warmth and comfort. So, follow your instincts and enjoy the charm of country life.

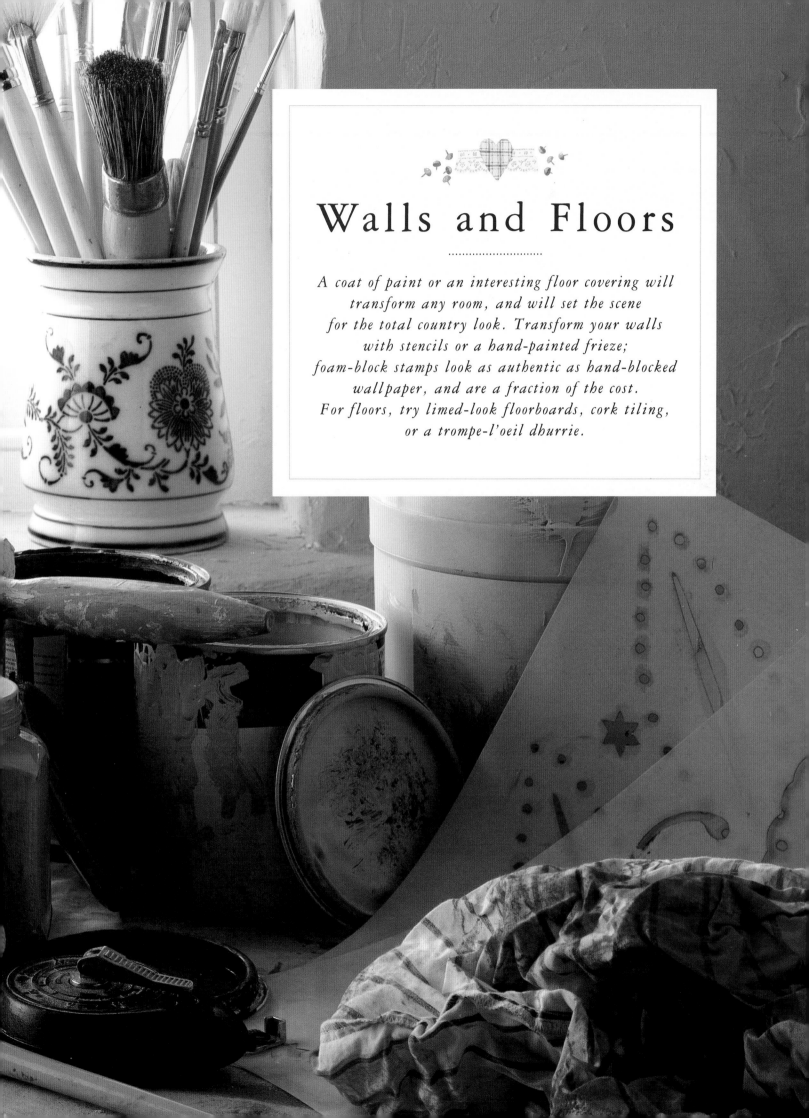

Walls and Floors

....

*A coat of paint or an interesting floor covering will
transform any room, and will set the scene
for the total country look. Transform your walls
with stencils or a hand-painted frieze;
foam-block stamps look as authentic as hand-blocked
wallpaper, and are a fraction of the cost.
For floors, try limed-look floorboards, cork tiling,
or a trompe-l'oeil dhurrie.*

The Country Palette

ABOVE: *Colours derived from nature are not necessarily sombre. Think of clear blue skies or a field of wildflowers.*

Colour has a great influence on us: it can affect our moods quite dramatically. Choose your palette from nature's harmonies, avoiding artificially brilliant colours. It would be a mistake to think that natural colours are all shades of beige; just think of autumn and the huge variety of yellows, oranges and scarlets that mingle among the trees.

When painting the walls country-style it is best to avoid a perfect, even finish – go instead for a patchy, glowing, colour-washed effect. By doing this you can use strong colour, but in a transparent way that is not as heavy as solid colour. Don't avoid strong colours like brick red, deep green or dusky blue. The furniture, rugs, pictures, ornaments, cushions and curtains will all combine to absorb the strength of the wall colour and dilute its power. If your rooms are dark, use the strong colours below dado-rail height only, with a creamy, light colour on the upper walls and ceiling. Darker colours can be very cosy in a large room, but if you want a room to look bigger it would be best to stick to a lighter scheme, and use a stencil or free-hand border to add colour and interest.

If mixing your own paint is too daunting a prospect, you could go for one of the new 'historic' ranges made by specialist producers. These paints are a lot more expensive than ordinary brands, but the colour ranges are designed to harmonize with antiques, natural building materials and old textiles, and if your budget can stretch to them, they really are wonderful.

If your courage fails and you choose white walls, think about highlighting the woodwork. Paint a deep, rich colour on the skirtings and the window- and door-frames, allow it to dry and then paint a light colour on top. Use a damp cloth to wipe off some of the topcoat, and sandpaper to lift colour that has dried. This will give you an effect of flashes of brilliance to add warmth to the room.

Choose natural colours that make you happy, and remember that country-style decorating is not about having everything matching. You don't need co-ordinating curtains, carpets and lampshades. On the contrary, the more eclectic the choice, the more stunning the effect can often be.

Giving your home the country look requires attention to the basics – the walls and floors. Get these right and the rest is easy. A bare room with powdery wall-paint, stencilling and a stripped, limed floor has a real country feeling, whereas no amount of folk artefacts and rustic furniture can transform to 'country' a tastefully wallpapered, corniced and thick-pile carpeted drawing room!

The ideal way to begin would be to clear the house, remove all the old wallpaper

and carpets and start from scratch, but this is a luxury that few can afford. It's more practical to think in terms of a room at a time, repainting the walls and adding one of the country-style floors that are featured in this chapter.

This chapter shows how the basic elements of a room can be changed to make it feel more individual. When you paint, stencil or print on your walls, they truly become your own, and this never happens with wallpaper, however good you are at hanging it! We sometimes suggest cheating a little: roughening up smooth surfaces, wiping off more paint than is put on, or stencilling unevenly, for a worn-away look. You can't wait a hundred years for this to occur naturally!

The ideas for the projects have been inspired by folk art and by real-life examples of country decorating of period homes. There has been a recent revival of interest in the subject and it is now possible to buy kits to age practically anything, with a plethora of equipment required for the job.

Whatever you choose for your walls and floor, it is important to see them in terms of a backdrop for your own tastes and possessions. Paintings, mirrors, lamps, plants, shelves, rugs and furniture will all add to the final effect. A painted border may appear to be too dominant in an empty room, but the effect will be much more subtle when the furnishings, accessories and personal details have been added.

Remember that country style is more about relaxation, comfort and harmony than precision and fashion; this is the type of decorating that is a pleasure to involve yourself in, so enjoy the process as well as the result.

CLOCKWISE FROM TOP LEFT: *The walls and floors have been coated with tinted varnish to simulate the patina of age.*
Deep, brick red is bold, yet warm in a sitting room. The soft colours of this crazy patchwork quilt
are punctuated with vibrant stitching.

Brushed-out Colour Glaze

This soft, patchy wall finish is pure country. It's traditionally achieved using either a very runny colour-wash, or an oil-based glaze tinted with oil colour, over eggshell paint. This project gives the same effect, but is easier to achieve.

The unusual element in the glaze is wallpaper paste, which is mixed in the usual way before the addition of PVA glue. The wallpaper paste adds a translucency to the colour and the PVA seals the surface when dry. To tint the glaze you can use powder, gouache or acrylic paint, mixed with a small amount of water first, so that it blends easily.

Use a large decorator's brush to apply the glaze, dabbing glaze on to the wall about five times within an arm's reach. Then use light, random strokes to sweep the glaze across the area, to use up the dabs and cover the area. Move along the wall, blending each area with the next.

This is a very cheap way of painting a room, so you can afford to mix up more glaze than you will use, and throw some away. This is preferable to running out before you finish, because it is so difficult to match the original colour. A litre / 1¾ pints of glaze will cover almost 40 square metres / yards.

MATERIALS

PVA glue
wallpaper paste
acrylic, gouache or powder paint,
to colour the glaze
large decorator's brush

1

Prepare your wall-surface: ideally it should be an off-white vinyl silk, but any plain, light colour will do, if it is clean. Wash old paint with sugar soap and leave it to dry. Mix up the glaze, using 1 part PVA glue, 5 parts water and ¼ part wallpaper paste. Tint it with three 20 cm / 8 in squirts from an acrylic or gouache tube, or about 15 ml / 1 tbsp of powder paint. Vary the intensity of colour to your own taste. Experiment on scrap lining paper painted with the same background colour as your walls. Get the feel of the glaze and brush, and adjust the colour at this stage if necessary.

2

Begin applying the glaze in an area of the room that will be hidden by furniture or pictures; as your technique improves you will be painting the more obvious areas. Start near the top of the wall, dabbing glaze on with the brush and then sweeping it over the surface with random strokes, as described previously.

3

The effect is streaky and the brushstrokes do show, but they can be softened before they are completely dry. After about 5 minutes brush the surface lightly with your brush but don't use any glaze. The brush will pick up any surplus glaze on the surface and leave a softer, less streaky effect. When working on edges and corners, apply the glaze and then brush it away from the corner or edge. You will still find that the colour may be more concentrated in some places, but it will all look very different when the room is furnished.

'Powdery' Paint Finish for Walls

You may need to 'rough-up' your walls a bit to achieve this look; this is easily done with a tub of filler, a spatula and some rough-grade sandpaper. Think of it as a reversal of the usual preparations!

This paint finish imitates the opaque, soft colour and powdery bloom of distemper, the wall finish most used before the invention of emulsion paint. The joy of decorating with this 'powdery finish' paint, is that it can be used directly on concrete, plaster or plasterboard – indeed almost any surface – without lining paper or special undercoats. The paint is diluted with water, to the consistency required, and is slapped on with a large brush. Mistakes and runs can be wiped off with a damp cloth, and the paint is a pleasure to use. It takes about two hours to dry, and the colour lightens considerably as it does so, until the final effect is revealed – a soft powdery surface of matt colour that will bring instant warmth to any room.

The 'distressed' plaster effect has a charmingly country feel. Perhaps we imagine that real country folk didn't have the time or inclination to decorate to a perfect finish; for whatever reasons, there is something very comfortable about walls with irregular surfaces and faded paint.

MATERIALS

*Polyfilla or similar filler
spatula
rough-grade sandpaper
Brats 'Mediterranean Palette'
paint in shade 'Asia'
large decorator's brush*

1

Prepare the walls by stripping off any wallpaper down to the bare plaster. Spread the filler irregularly with the spatula to simulate the uneven texture of old plaster. Use thin layers, applied randomly from different directions. Don't worry about overdoing the effect; you can always rub it back with sandpaper when it's dry, after about an hour.

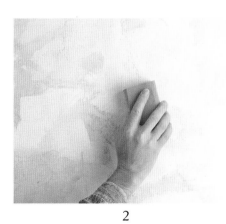

2

Blend the dried filler into the original wall surface using the sandpaper, leaving rougher areas for a more obvious distressed effect. Mix the paint with water in the ratio 2 parts water to 1 part paint.

3

Begin painting at ceiling height. The paint is likely to splash a bit, so protect any surfaces with an old sheet or decorator's cloth. Use the paintbrush in a random way, rather than in straight lines, and expect a patchy effect – it will fade as the paint dries. The second coat needs to be stronger, so use less water in the mixture. Stir the paint well; it should have the consistency of single cream.

Apply the second coat in the same way, working the brush into any cracks or rough plaster areas. Two hours later the 'bloom' of the powdery finish will have appeared. The element of surprise makes decorating with this paint exciting, especially as the final texture is so mellow and effective at covering, but not concealing, the irregularities of the wall's surface. We used this surface as a base for the stencilled border on the following page.

Stencilled Border

Stencilling tends to spread around the house like a climbing plant, appearing round doorways and winding along picture rails, up staircases and across floors! It is a delightful and habit-forming activity and it's extremely difficult to be a minimalist when it comes to stencilling.

The design used for this border came from a Rhode Island house that was built and decorated in the eighteenth century. Stencilling was an extremely popular means of decorating interiors, and stencils were used to create pillars and friezes as well as all-over patterns, with as many as seven different designs on a single wall.

A border design like this one is perfectly suited for use above a dado-rail, but there is no reason why you should not use it at picture-rail, or skirting-board height, or even as a frame around a window. Or you may not have a dado-rail but still like the

effect of a wall divided in this way. In this case it is a simple matter of marking the division with paint or varnish.

Use a plumb-line and a long ruler to divide the wall, marking the line in pencil. The wall below the line can be painted a darker shade, or, if you are using the 'Mediterranean Palette' colour, a coat of clear satin varnish will darken the colour and add a sheen. The stencilled border will visually integrate the two sections of wall and soften the edges between them. If you vary the depth of stencilled colour, it will look naturally faded by time.

MATERIALS

tracing paper
Mylar or stencil card
spray adhesive
scalpel or craft knife
masking tape
Brats Mediterranean Palette paint
in shade 'Asia' (optional)
varnish in shade 'Antique Pine'
household paintbrush
stencil paint
stencil brush

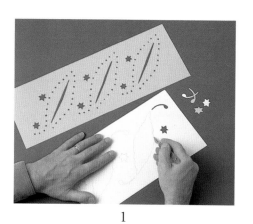

1

Trace and enlarge the pattern from the template section. Stick it on the Mylar using spray adhesive. Use a scalpel or craft knife to cut out the stencil carefully. Repair any mistakes with masking tape and always use a very sharp blade which will give you the most control when cutting. Peel off the remaining tracing paper.

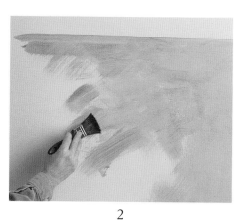

2

If desired, prepare the powdery paint finish on the previous page, then paint the whole wall in 'Asia'. Paint the lower half of the wall with a coat of Antique Pine tinted varnish. Use random brush strokes for a rough finish.

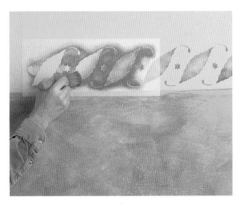

3

Apply a light spray of adhesive to the back of
the stencil and leave it to dry for 5 minutes.
Position the stencil at a corner and paint the
first colour. Use the paint very sparingly,
wiping the brush on absorbent kitchen paper
before using it on the wall. You can always
go over a light area to darken it later, but
excess paint on the brush will cause blobs,
and bleed through to the back of the stencil.
Lift the stencil and wipe any excess paint
from the pattern edges before positioning it
alongside the stencilling. Continue along
the top of the dado-rail until the first colour
is complete.

4

Stencil paint is fast-drying, so you can
immediately begin to add the next colour,
starting at the same point as you did with the
first. Work your way around the border,
remembering to wipe the stencil clean
as you go.

Free-hand Frieze with Half-gloss to Dado Height

This project combines the idea of dividing up the wall with textures and colours, and the free-hand painting of a vine frieze. The frieze will take some planning and preparation to achieve the casual free-hand effect, but the finished painting will look effortless and be unique.

A coat of gloss paint below the dado-rail will provide a practical, tough, wipe-clean surface where you most need it, and the gloss gives the colour a marvellous reflective shine. The lighter colour above the dado has a matt texture and the shade is reminiscent of cream straight from the dairy. If you don't have a dado-rail dividing your wall, this project is just as effective on a plain wall.

The secret of painting free-hand curves on a vertical surface, is to steady your hand on a mahlstick, which is quite simply a piece of dowel about 45 cm / 18 in long. Make a small pad of cotton wool at one end, cover it with a small square of cotton or muslin and secure it with a rubber band. Use the stick by pressing the pad against the wall with your spare hand, holding the stick free of the wall. Rest your brush hand lightly on it to prevent wobbles and jerks. Practise the curves with the mahlstick before starting the frieze, but remember that the charm of hand-painting is its variability, so relax and enjoy yourself.

MATERIALS

National Trust paint in shades 51 (Sudbury Yellow) emulsion, 14 (Berrington Blue) full gloss and 43 (Eating Room Red) oil eggshell paint-roller and tray gloss-roller 2.5 cm / 1 in decorator's brush masking tape, if necessary chalk line or ruler chalk stencil card with design

medium-weight card scalpel or craft knife 1 cm / ½ in square-ended artist's brush gouache paint in Indian red and raw sienna 45 cm / 18 in length of dowelling (of pencil thickness) small wad of cotton wool square of cotton fabric rubber band number 6 round-ended artist's brush

1

Apply yellow emulsion to the prepared wall with the paint-roller, from ceiling to dado. Paint blue gloss colour between the dado and skirting, using the gloss-roller. Using the red eggshell paint, and the 2.5 cm / 1 in brush, paint the skirting board and the dado-rail, if you have one. Use masking tape, if necessary, to give a clean line. Use a chalk line or ruler to draw light chalk guide-lines, marking out the depth of the frieze.

2

Using your chosen stencil, lightly mark out the position of the frieze by drawing through the stencil.

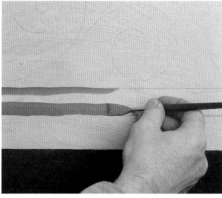

3

Paint the thick and thin lines, using the square-ended brush, flat and on its side, and the gouache paints. To add variety to the line, mix up two different shades of the same colour and use both randomly.

4

Make up your mahlstick as described on the previous page.

5

Paint in the curved stems, using the round-ended brush and gouache, supporting your hand on the mahlstick. Try to make your movements as fluid as possible.

6

Add the bunches of grapes, above and below the stems using the round-ended brush. Overlap the double lines in some places: remember that you are aiming for a hand-painted look, not a regular-repeat pattern.

Foam-block Painting

Printing with cut-out foam blocks must be the easiest possible way to achieve the effect of hand-blocked wallpaper, and it gives an irregularity of pattern that is impossible in machine-produced papers. Another special feature of this project is the paint that we have used – a combination of wallpaper paste, PVA glue and gouache colour. This is not only cheap, but it also has a wonderful translucent quality all of its own. The combination of sponge and paint works well, because pressing and lifting the sponge emphasizes the texture that results from using a slightly sticky paint.

The best foam for cutting is high in density but still soft, such as upholsterer's foam; it needs to be at least 2.5 cm / 1 in thick. You need to be able to hold the foam firmly without distorting the printing surface.

Paint some of your background colour on to sheets of scrap paper, and then use this to try out your sponge-printing; use different densities and combinations of colour, making a note of the proportions of colour to paste in each one. This

means you will be able to mix up the same colour in a larger amount when you print on the wall (although the paint will go a very long way). The background used here is painted using the brushed-out colour glaze described on page 16.

MATERIALS

tracing paper, if necessary
upholsterer's foam off-cuts
felt-tipped pen
scalpel or craft knife
plumb-line
paper square measuring
15 × 15 cm / 6 × 6 in, or
according to your chosen spacing
wallpaper paste
PVA glue
gouache paint or ready-mixed
watercolour paint in viridian,
deep green and off-white
saucer
clear matt varnish (optional)

1

Photocopy or trace the design from the template section and cut out the shapes to leave a stencil. Trace the design on to the foam and outline it using a felt-tipped pen.

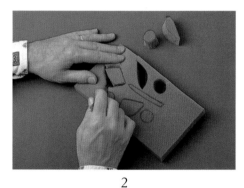

2

Cut out the shapes using a sharp scalpel or craft knife: first cut around the pattern, and then part the foam slightly and cut through the entire thickness.

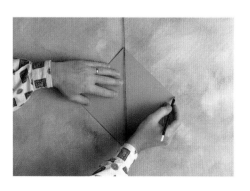

3

Attach the plumb-line to the wall/ceiling join in one corner. Now turn the square sheet of paper on the diagonal and let the plumb-line fall through the centre, lining up the top and bottom corners with the line. Make pencil dots on the wall at each corner. Move the square down the line, marking the corner points each time. Then move the line along sideways. Continue until the whole wall is marked with a grid of dots.

4

Mix wallpaper paste and water according to the manufacturer's instructions. Add PVA glue, in the proportion 3 parts paste to 1 part PVA. Add a squeeze of viridian and deep green gouache paint or ready-mixed watercolour, and blend the ingredients until well mixed. Test the mixture on scrap paper, adding more colour if necessary.

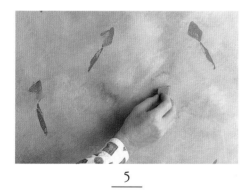

5

Put some paint into a saucer and dip the first sponge into it. Wipe off excess paint, and then print with the sponge using a light rolling motion. Lift and print again, using the pencil dots as a positioning guide.

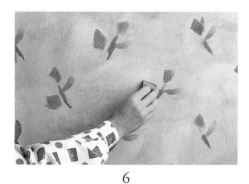

6

Use the second sponge to complete the sprig design with leaf shapes, varying the position slightly to add life.

7

Use the dot-shaped sponge and the off-white colour to complete the motif with berries, adding the colour to the PVA mixture as before. Go over the leaves or stalks on some sprigs and let others 'float' alongside. If your walls are to be exposed to steam or splashes, or even fingerprints, you may like to protect this finish with a coat of clear matt varnish.

'Limed' Floorboards

Liming sanded wooden floorboards gives a much softer impression than stains or tinted varnishes, reminiscent of scrubbed pine kitchen-tables, washed-out wooden spoons, or driftwood bleached by the sun and the sea. If you are lucky enough to possess a sandable floor, try this easy alternative to time-consuming conventional liming. The floor can be a traditional off-white, or tinted to any pastel shade.

Raking-out the grain with a wire brush makes the channels for the paint, as well as clearing out any residual polish or varnish. If you like the wood grain to show as much as possible, wipe the surface with a damp cloth before it dries; the colour will then be concentrated in the raked-out grain of the floorboards. When the floor is dry, a coat of acrylic floor varnish will seal the colour.

MATERIALS

coarse wire brush
white emulsion paint
acrylic paint in raw umber
large decorator's brush
clean damp cloth
clear matt varnish

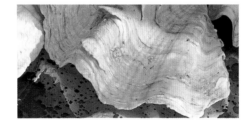

1

Use a wire brush to rake-out the wood following the grain direction at all times. Brush and vacuum the floor very carefully.

2

Mix up the wash, using 3 parts of water to 1 part of emulsion. Tint the colour with raw umber acrylic, or, if you prefer, use a pastel colour: pink, blue, green or yellow will all look good in the right setting, and very little of the actual colour will show. Experiment on spare boards.

3

Apply the wash with the decorator's brush, beginning in a corner at the skirting board and following the direction of the grain to the other edge.

4

Use a damp cloth to wipe away any excess paint and reveal the grain. A wet cloth will just wash away the paint, so keep it just damp for this. When the floor is completely dry, apply several coats of varnish to protect and seal the surface, allowing plenty of drying time between each coat.

Hardboard Floor with Trompe-l'œil Dhurrie

*It is a sad fact that not every home is blessed with handsome floorboards, to be
sanded and waxed to a golden gleam. Most older houses have a mixture of new
and old boards that aren't good enough to be made into a feature.*

Hardboard can be a surprisingly attractive solution if you're faced with a low budget and a patchy selection of floorboards. The utilitarian appearance of hardboard means it is most often used as a levelling surface below vinyl; used in its own right, however, and decorated with stencils, it can look very stylish.

To counteract the potential drabness of a large area of hardboard this project shows how to paint a trompe-l'œil dhurrie in the centre of the room, so that the plain board becomes the border for the dhurrie. Hardboard provides a wonderfully smooth surface for painting and the dhurrie will provide a focal point that is guaranteed to be a talking point as well!

MATERIALS

newspaper
hardboard to fit the floor area
small hammer
panel pins
Stanley knife
ruler
tape measure
Crown Compatibles emulsion paint in shades 'Dusky Blue', 'Splash Blue' and 'Regency Cream'
2.5 cm / 1 in square-ended brush
acrylic paint in dark blue and black
decorator's brushes
masking tape
stencil card or Mylar
scalpel or craft knife
2 cm / ½ in stencil brush
clear matt varnish

1

Lay sheets of newspaper on the floor to make an even surface. Fit the first sheet of hardboard into the corner nearest the door. Hammer in panel pins 7.5 cm / 3 in apart and 1.5 cm / ⅝ in in from the edge and fasten the hardboard to the existing floor.

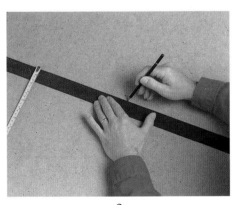

2

Lay the next sheet of hardboard alongside the first, butting it hard up against the first sheet, and right up to the skirting board. Continue laying the whole boards across the room until you reach the point at which the hardboard needs to be trimmed to fit. Measure the space, at least twice, if it is not too large or awkwardly shaped; if it is irregularly shaped, make a newsprint pattern to be sure of getting a good fit. Cut the hardboard using a Stanley knife and a ruler on the shiny side, then breaking along the cut.

3

If you decide to place your dhurrie in the centre of the room, use a tape measure to find the centre line, and then measure out from it. The dhurrie can be as large or small as you like; this rug is made up of units 150 × 75 cm / 5 × 2½ feet, which you can multiply or divide to suit your room size. Mark the outline of the dhurrie on the floor. Outline the area with the square-ended brush and then fill in the Dusky Blue colour. Leave to dry for 2 hours.

4

Tint the blue to a darker shade by adding a squeeze of black acrylic, and then paint over the area with a dryish brush, to give the dhurrie a woven texture.

. . . continued

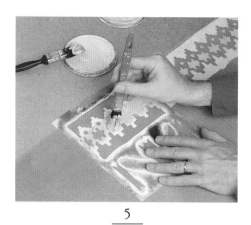

5

Trace and cut out the stencil design from the template section. Mask off the outer patterns with tape. Position the stencil 2 cm / ¾ in from the edge, and stencil the central design in Splash Blue emulsion. Remove the tape and clean the stencil.

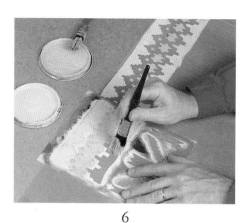

6

Now mask off the central pattern and stencil the pattern on either side in Regency Cream emulsion.

7

Position the medallion stencil along the edge of the border and paint all the pattern, except for the outermost lines, in dark blue acrylic. You can mask off these lines with tape, as in the previous steps.

8

Mask off the central medallion and stencil the outer lines cream.

9

Soften the dark blue of the central medallions with light dabs of Splash Blue emulsion.

10

Apply at least two coats of clear varnish to the whole area.

Cork-tile Chequer-board Floor

Cork is a wonderful natural material that provides a warm, quiet and relatively cheap floor-covering. It has been largely confined to the kitchen and bathroom in the past, but should not be overlooked when choosing a floor for living areas.

It is important to lay cork tiles on an even surface, so tack a layer of hardboard across the floorboards first. Use only floor-grade cork tiles. The unsealed tiles used here absorbed the coloured varnish well; two coats of clear polyurethane varnish with a satin finish gave a protective seal. You may prefer a proprietary brand of cork tile sealant.

MATERIALS

*cork floor tiles
wood-stains in shades 'Dark Jacobean Oak' and 'Antique Pine'
large decorator's brush
cork-tile adhesive, if necessary
clear satin varnish*

1

Paint half of the tiles with the Dark Jacobean Oak wood-stain and the remaining tiles with the Antique Pine wood-stain and leave them to dry overnight. Measure the floor length to establish the number of Jacobean Oak tiles needed and cut half that number in half diagonally. Begin laying tiles in the corner that will be seen most; then, if you have to trim a tile at the other end, it will not be so obvious. If you are using self-adhesive tiles, simply peel off the backing.

2

Lay the contrasting tiles next, tight up against the first row, wiping off any excess adhesive that has been forced up between the tiles, if you're using adhesive. Once you have laid the two rows, measure the nearest adjoining wall and cut half-tiles to fit the length of that skirting as well. Stick these down.

3

Now, work to fill the floor space diagonally. Trim the tiles at the opposite edge to fit snugly against the skirting board. Apply two coats of clear varnish to seal the floor. It is important to make sure that the first coat is bone-dry before you apply the next one, so be patient, and let it dry overnight.

Acorn and Oak-leaf Border

A painted border can offset the austerity of plain wooden floorboards, while the pattern links different areas without dominating the room. The scale of the oak-leaf pattern can be adjusted to suit the size of your room, but try to 'think big' and enlarge the design to at least four times larger than life size, otherwise the impact will be lost.

Acorns and oak leaves have been used to decorate homes for hundreds of years, and they have a special place in country decorating. William Morris, the famous designer of the Arts and Crafts movement, used many country trees and plants in his patterns, and designed a wonderful wallpaper called 'Acorns'. Let the old saying 'Tall oaks from little acorns grow' be your inspiration, and use this painted-floor border as the basis for a warm and welcoming country-style living room.

Paint the background a dark colour and use paint with a matt finish as this will 'hold' your outline drawings better than a smooth or glossy paint. Begin at the corners and work towards the middle, using the templates as a measuring guide to work out your spacing. Once you have planned the placing of your design, work on a 60 cm / 24 in area at a time, using your whole arm to make the curves, not just the wrist. This way your painting will flow in a more natural way.

MATERIALS

medium-weight card
spray adhesive
scalpel or craft knife
masking tape
ruler
set square
National Trust paint in shade 'Off Black'
decorator's brush
white chinagraph pencil or chalk
white plate
gouache paint in yellow, sienna, umber, etc.
soft artist's brush
plank or long ruler
lining brush
clear matt varnish

2

Beginning at the corner, draw around the oak-leaf template with the chinagraph pencil or chalk. Add stems or acorns to make the pattern fit around the corner, and then continue along the border. Use the template as a measuring guide, to make sure that the design fits comfortably.

1

Use a photocopier to enlarge the oak-leaf and acorn pattern from the template section to at least four times life size (larger if you have a big room). Stick the enlargement on to medium-weight card and cut around the shape with scalpel or craft knife, to leave a cardboard template. Use masking tape, with a ruler and set square to outline the dark background colour. Apply the colour using the decorator's brush and leave to dry.

3

Using a white plate as a palette, squeeze out several different tones of yellow, sienna, umber, etc. Mix them as you paint; this adds variety.

4

Fill in the oak-leaf shapes, using subtle variations in colour for added interest.

5

Add the finishing touches and flourishes like the leaf veining, stems and acorns.

6

Use a straight edge, such as a plank, and a lining brush to paint the lines that enclose the border about 2.5 cm / 1 in from the edge. Apply 3–4 coats of clear varnish, allowing generous drying time (overnight if possible) between coats.

Painted Canvas Floorcloth

Canvas floorcloths were first used by the early American settlers, who had travelled across the sea from Europe. They recycled canvas sailcloth, painting it to imitate the oriental carpets that were popular with the rich merchants and aristocrats in their native lands. Many layers of linseed oil were applied to the painted canvas to make them waterproof and hard-wearing.

The floorcloths were superseded by linoleum, and, unfortunately, few good old examples remain; they had no intrinsic value and were discarded when worn. Recently, however, they have undergone something of a revival. With the tough modern varnishes now available, they provide an unusual and hard-wearing alternative to the ubiquitous oriental rug.

The design for this floorcloth is based on a nineteenth-century quilt pattern called 'Sun, Moon and Stars'. The original quilt was made in very bright primary colours, but more muted shades work well for the floorcloth.

MATERIALS

craft knife or pair of sharp scissors
heavy artist's canvas (to order from art supply shops)
pencil
ruler
strong fabric adhesive
drawing pin and 1 m / 1 yd length of string
cardboard
acrylic paints in red, blue and green
medium-size square-ended artist's brush
medium-sized pointed artist's brush
varnish in shade 'Antique Pine'
household paintbrush
medium-grade sandpaper

1

Cut the canvas to the size required, allowing an extra 4 cm / 1½ in all around. Draw a 4 cm / 1½ in wide border around the edge of the canvas and mitre the corners. Apply fabric adhesive to the border and fold it flat.

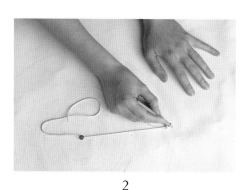

2

Referring to the diagram in the template section, find the centre-point of the canvas and secure the string to the drawing pin at this point. You will now be able to draw the five circles needed for the design, by holding a pencil at various distances along the length of the tautly pulled string. Keep the tension on the string to draw a perfect circle.

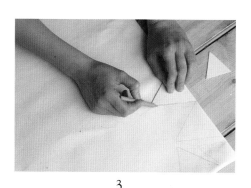

3

Cut three differently sized cardboard triangles to make the saw-toothed edges of the two circles and the outside border. Just move the triangle along the pencil guidelines using the card as a template to draw around.

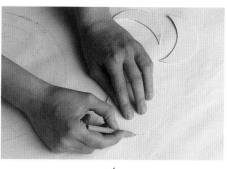

4

Cut a card circle to make a template for the full moons and draw them in position. Then trim the circle to make the crescent and then the sickle moons, drawing them in position. Do the same for the stars.

5

Now start filling in the red. Use the flat-ended brush for larger areas and the pointed brush for outlines and fine work.

6

Fill in the pale blue and green circles of colour.

7

Apply 3–4 coats of Antique Pine varnish with a clean household brush, rubbing down each dried coat with sandpaper before applying the next one. Overnight drying is best.

Furniture and Furnishings

Hand-painted furniture is all part of the country look, but unless you have the luck to inherit beautiful old pieces they often remain a distant dream. However, there are still bargains to be had from junk shops and flea markets, and they can be transformed fairly inexpensively. Renovate a table with a colourful border, line a chair for a French country kitchen, or create your own shelves or kitchen dresser.

Country-style Motifs and Patterns

There are three main sources of motifs in country style – nature, local tradition and religion. Nature and the elements are the strongest influences of all and are celebrated in the decoration of rural homes throughout the world. Flowers and foliage vary according to climate; this is reflected in patterns and motifs, although some plants, like the vine for instance, have been used decoratively since classical times and are found in the art of many cultures.

Many fruit, flower and foliage motifs have symbolic meanings too, and these were incorporated into homes for their protective value in warding off evil, or for the bringing of good fortune. The rose is used as a symbol of love, both divine and earthly, and the tulip stands for prosperity. The oak leaf and acorn are associated with great potential and the future, while ivy symbolizes tenacity. The sunflower radiates warmth and is guaranteed to bring thoughts of summer to winter days.

Animals, birds and fish feature as well. Wild creatures, farm animals, faithful pets and feathered friends all find their way into country crafts and patterns. The rooster has been used since early Christian times as a symbol of faith, but it is more likely to feature in country

ABOVE: *The tulip is a popular folk motif, and symbolizes prosperity.*

decorating in celebration of his great decorative shape, coupled with his early-morning tyranny.

Cats and dogs are often commemorated in embroideries or paintings, as are horses and other farmyard friends. Patchwork quilts feature many animal and fruit designs that have been stylized to great effect, and this, in turn, has created a style of stencilling whose origins are the quilt-maker's patterns rather than the original inspiration.

Religious influences are especially noticeable in Roman Catholic countries, where there is more emphasis on the visual celebration of faith. Shrines, altars, festive decorations and votive offerings are all a part of the decoration of rural homes in countries like Mexico, Spain, Italy and France.

Harvest motifs, like the wheat sheaf or the cornucopia are popular in most cultures. Fruits have been incorporated into woven and printed textiles, and vegetables are a favourite subject in 'theorem' paintings, a style of stencil paintings used in American folk art.

One of the most common country motifs is the heart: whether punched out of tin, carved out of planks or stencilled on to walls, the heart is everywhere. It symbolizes love and it is a uniquely simple and adaptable motif. The shape hardly changes at all, yet it can be used in many different ways without diminishing its effect. The heart has been used for many centuries across many cultures, and yet there still seems to be an infinite number of new ways to use it.

Geometric shapes have been borrowed from patchwork quilts, and suns, moons and stars will always be popular motifs. They are universal.

The beauty of country-style decorating is the nonchalance with which motifs, styles and patterns can be mixed. The only decorative effect to be avoided is mass-produced adulterated versions of country-style designs, because they will have lost their heart and soul in the manufacturing process!

LEFT: *Decorative surface detail is characteristic of country style, as in this free-hand painted box.*

RIGHT: *The heart, a perennial favourite, is appliquéd in a repeat pattern on this patchwork piece.*

CLOCKWISE FROM TOP LEFT: *Stencilled details give this chair a look of pure country. Geometric patterns are always popular choices for textiles. The free-hand, organic design on this box is inspired by nature. A tin heart is decorated with punched geometric patterns.*

Painted Table

It is still possible, thank goodness, to find bargain tables in junk shops, and this one cost less than a tenth of the price of a new one. It is the sort of table that you can imagine standing in a country cottage parlour, covered with a lace-edged cloth and laden with tea-time treats. There is no guarantee that you will find a similar table, but any old table could be decorated in the same way.

Before you decorate your bargain, you may have to strip off the old paint or varnish and treat it for wood-worm, as we did. Any serious holes can be filled with wood-filler and then sanded and stained to match. The trick is to emphasize the good features and play down the bad. Old table-tops look more interesting than new ones and are well worth sanding, bleaching and staining. The stain on the table legs contrasts well with the red and green paint used on the table-top. The lining can be attempted free-hand, but masking tape makes the job much easier. Mark the position lightly in pencil so that all the lines are the same distance from the edge.

MATERIALS

*table
wood-stain in shade 'Dark Jacobean Oak'
household paintbrush
emulsion paint in red and green
1 cm / ½ in square-ended artist's brush
masking tape
shellac
beeswax polish
soft clean cloth*

1

Prepare and treat the table as necessary. Use a rag to rub the wood-stain into the table legs, applying more as it is absorbed into the wood. The finish should be an even, almost black tone.

2

Paint the base of the table-top with red emulsion.

3

Measure 5 cm / 2 in in from the edge of the table and place a strip of masking tape this distance in from each of the edges. Leave a 2 cm / ¾ in gap and then place the next strips of tape to run parallel with the first set.

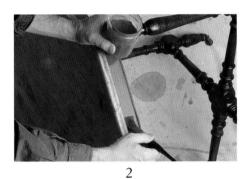

4

Fill in the strip between the tape with the green paint and leave to dry.

5

Apply two coats of shellac to the table.

6

Finish the table with a coat of beeswax
polish, buffing it to a warm sheen with a soft
clean cloth.

Painted Bench

*Every home should have a bench like this, to squeeze extra guests around the
dinner table and to keep by the back door for comfortable boot-changing.
This bench was made by a carpenter, from a photograph seen in a book of
old country furniture. The wood is reclaimed floorboards, which give just the
right rustic feel to the bench.*

The decoration is applied in a rough
folk-art style that adds a touch of
humour. You can use this style to
decorate any bench, and even a plain
modern design will lose its hard edges
and take on the character of a piece of
rustic hand-made furniture.

MATERIALS

*bench
medium-grade sandpaper
shellac
household paintbrushes
emulsion paint in deep red,*

*dark blue-grey and light
blue-green
small piece of sponge
varnish in shade 'Antique Pine'
clear matt varnish*

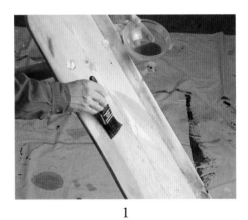

1

Sand the bare wood and seal it with a
coat of shellac.

2

Paint the legs in dark blue-grey emulsion,
working directly on to the wood.

3

Paint the seat with the
deep red emulsion.

4

Use the sponge to dab an even pattern of
blue-green spots across the whole surface of
the seat.

5

When the paint is dry, rub the seat and edges
with sandpaper, to simulate the wear and tear
of a thousand harvest suppers.

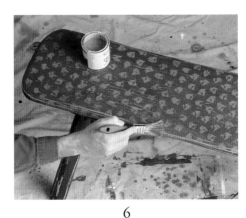

6

Apply one coat of Antique Pine varnish to
the whole bench. Then apply two more coats
of matt varnish for a strong finish.

Shaker-inspired Peg Rail

The Shakers were a religious movement whose ideals inspired a style of furnishings and furniture of great simplicity and beauty of form. They did not believe in ornamentation or decoration for its own sake, but held that functional objects should be as beautiful and as well made as possible. The name 'Shaker' comes from the ecstatic movements that occurred in their worship.

Peg rails were very characteristic of Shaker homes, and were used for hanging all kinds of utensils and even chairs, keeping the floor clear. Our rail is a very inexpensive and simplified version of the Shaker idea, and what it lacks in fine craftsmanship it makes up for in practicality. We have used a pine plank, with a sawn-up broom-handle to make the pegs. These rails work well all around the house, but are especially useful in hallways, children's rooms and bathrooms. The coat of paint is not strictly Shaker in style, but will disguise the rail's humble origins.

MATERIALS

pine plank 2.5 cm / 1 in thick
ruler
saw
plane
drill with bit for broom-
handle holes
1 or 2 broom-handles
medium-grade sandpaper
wood glue

wooden block and hammer
shellac
household paintbrushes
Crown Compatibles emulsion
paint in shade 'Dusky Blue'
varnish in shade 'Antique Pine'
white spirit, if necessary
spirit-level
rawl plugs and long screws

1

Measure and cut the wood to the length required. Plane it to smooth and round the edges.

2

Mark the peg positions 20 cm / 8 in apart along the length. The spacing can be altered to suit your requirements.

3

Drill holes 1.5 cm / ⅝ in deep in which to recess the pegs.

4

Cut up the broom-handles into 13 cm / 5 in lengths. Sand the edges to round them off.

5

Apply wood glue and fit the pegs into their holes using a small wooden block and hammer to fit them securely.

6

Apply one coat of shellac to seal the surface of the wood.

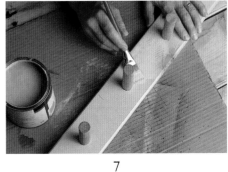

7

Paint the rail blue.

8

Use medium-grade sandpaper to rub back to bare wood along the edges.

9

Give the whole shelf a coat of Antique Pine varnish. Dip a rag in white spirit (for polyurethane varnish) or water (for acrylic varnish) and rub off some of the varnish. Use a spirit-level and ruler to mark the position of the rail on the wall. Drill holes through the rail at 40 cm / 18 in intervals. Drill into the wall, using suitable wall-fixings and screws.

Painted and Lined Country Chair

It is always worth buying interesting individual chairs when you spot them, as they are often very inexpensive if they need 'doing up'. Four mismatching chairs painted the same way will make a convincing and charming set, and the effect is pure country.

This is a typical French, country-style, rush-seated chair, with curvaceous lines just begging to be accentuated with lining. The essentials of sturdiness and comfort have not been ignored, the seat is generously woven and it is very comfortable. (It is always worth sitting on your chair before you buy because it may have been custom-made for a differently shaped person!)

Colour is a real revitalizer and we have chosen a yellow and blue colour scheme reminiscent of the painter Monet's kitchen, to bring out the French character of the chair. It is worth spending time preparing the wood, and this may mean stripping all the paint if there are several layers of gloss. If you do have the chair professionally stripped, the joints will need to be re-glued, because the caustic stripper dissolves glue as well as paint.

MATERIALS

country-style chair
medium-grade sandpaper
undercoat
household paintbrushes
shellac and wood primer,
if necessary
Crown Satinwood paint in yellow
wire wool
hard pencil
tube of artist's oil colour in
ultramarine blue
white spirit
long-haired square-ended
artist's brush
varnish in shade 'Antique Pine'

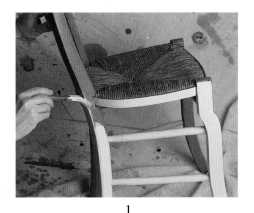

1

If the chair hasn't been stripped, rub it down well with medium-grade sandpaper. Apply the undercoat, or if the chair has been stripped, give it a coat of shellac followed by wood primer. Paint the chair yellow.

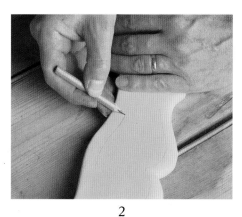

2

When this coat has dried, use wire wool to rub the paint back along the edges where natural wearing away would take place. With a pencil draw the lining, following the curves of the chair.

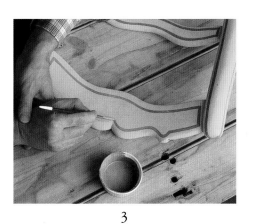

3

Mix the oil paint with white spirit in the proportions 3 parts paint to 1 part white spirit. You need paint that flows smoothly from the brush and allows you to retain control. If you find the paint too runny, add more colour. Practise the brushstroke with the artist's brush on scrap paper or board, supporting your brush-hand with your spare hand. Controlling your lines is a matter of confidence, which grows as you paint. Paint the lining on the legs, chairback and seat.

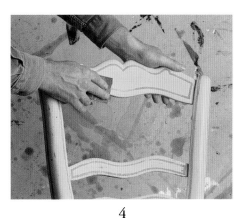

4

When dry, rub back with wire wool in places, as you did with the yellow.

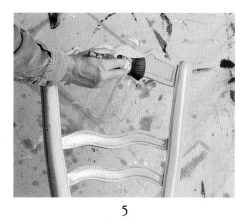

5

Finally apply a coat or two of varnish to soften the colour and protect the lining.

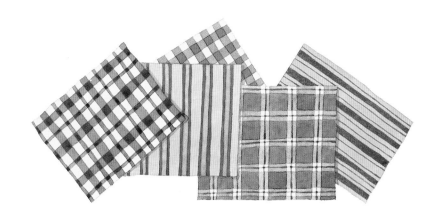

Pie-safe Cupboard

Cupboards like this one were mainly used in America as cooling cupboards for freshly baked goods. The doors were made out of decoratively punched and pierced tin sheets that allowed the delicious aromas to waft out, but prevented flies from getting in. They were called 'safes' because they were fitted with locks to keep temptation out of reach of little fingers lured by delicious smells!

We used an existing old pine cupboard to make the pie-safe, replacing the wooden front panels with newly pierced tin ones. Milled-steel sheet can be bought from sheet-metal suppliers, or try asking at a hardware store or looking in Yellow Pages. Care must be taken, as the edges of the sheet are very sharp, and need to be folded over to make a safe seam. You can crimp or flatten the edges using pliers.

The actual patterning is done with a hammer and nail, or, for more linear piercing, you can use a small chisel. This pattern is our own interpretation of a traditional design, but once you begin, your own style will emerge. You may find other ways of making patterns, perhaps using the end of a Phillips screwdriver, for instance – really anything goes. If the cupboard is to be used in the kitchen, add a protective backing sheet behind the tin, to cover the sharp edges. To get rid of the very new gleam of pierced metal, rub vinegar into the surface.

MATERIALS

old cupboard with one or two panelled doors
tracing paper
medium-grade sandpaper
shellac, if necessary
24- or 26-gauge milled-steel sheet(s) to fit (allow 1 cm / ½ in all around for the seams)
pliers and tinsnips, if necessary
masking tape

pair of compasses or transfer paper
chinagraph pencil
hammer
selection of different nails, screwdrivers and chisels
backing material such as hardboard, if necessary
panel pins
varnish in shade 'Antique Pine'
household paintbrush

1

Remove any beading and ease out the existing panels from the cupboard doors. Measure the space and use tracing paper to plan the design to fit. Rub down the cupboard with sandpaper. If it has been stripped, re-seal it with a coat of shellac. Trim the metal sheet, if necessary. Fold over the sharp edge of the metal sheet, to make a seam about 1 cm / ½ in deep around the edge. Crimp firmly with pliers. Put masking tape over sharp edges, to prevent accidental cuts.

2

Transfer your design on to the tin surface, using a pair of compasses. If you find this tricky, trace the whole design and use transfer paper to put it on to the metal. Add any extra designs with the chinagraph pencil.

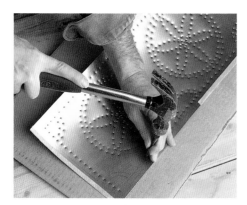

3

Practise piercing on a scrap of tin, such as a biscuit-tin lid, so that you know how hard you need to hit the nail to pierce a hole, and also how just to dent the surface without piercing it. Place thick cardboard or an old towel or blanket beneath the tin to absorb the noise and protect the surface underneath. Once you are confident with the hammer and nail, or whatever tool you want to use, hammer out the pattern.

4

Fit the pierced panels, and the backing if you are using it, into the door and replace the beading to secure it. Use short panel pins at a distance of 4 cm / 1½ in apart, all around the panel to fix in place.

5

Sandpaper the edges to simulate a time-worn effect. Give the wood a protective coat of antiquing varnish.

Shelf with Hanging Hooks

This large shelf with a backboard and hooks would suit a kitchen, entrance hall or large bathroom. It is really simple to make, requiring only the most basic of carpentry skills and tools. The shelf can be painted or varnished, depending on the wood, and it's a really handsome and useful piece of furniture.

The very best wood to use is reclaimed pine, usually floorboards. Demolition or builder's reclamation yards usually have stocks of old wood, but be prepared to pay more for old than new pine. If you're leaving the shelf unpainted it's definitely worth the extra money for old wood. If you intend to paint the shelf, new wood can be used for the backing board, to cut down on the price.

The best feature of the shelf is the very generously sized brackets, which were copied from an old farm storeroom. They have been cut from a section of old pine door, using a jig-saw. The brackets will support the shelf and balance the weight, but the shelf should be screwed into a sound brick wall, using suitable rawl plugs and long steel screws.

This type of shelf is very popular in rural eastern European communities. The hooks can either be new brass or wrought-iron coathooks; or you may be lucky enough to find an old set. Either way they are bound to be concealed, as hooks usually attract more than they were ever intended to hold!

MATERIALS

tracing paper
piece of pine 34 cm × 18 cm ×
3 cm / 14½ in × 7 in × 1¼ in
thick, for the brackets
jig-saw
drill with No. 5 and 6 bits
pine plank 100 cm × 15 cm ×
2 cm / 3 ft 4 in × 6 in × ¾ in
thick, for the backboard
pine plank 130 cm × 22 cm ×
2 cm / 4 ft 4 in × 8½ in × ¾ in
thick, for the shelf
wood glue
wood-screws
shellac
household paintbrush
2.5 cm / 1 in brush
Crown Compatibles emulsion
paint in shades 'Dusky Blue',
'Aqua Spring', and 'Precious Jade'
clean damp cloth
wire wool
medium-grade sandpaper
6 coathooks
rawl plugs, if necessary
3 long screws

1

Trace the bracket pattern from the template section and enlarge it until the longest side measures 33.5 cm / 13½ in. Trace this on to the wood, fitting it into one corner, and then flip the pattern over and trace it again into the opposite-end corner. The two can be cut out at the same time, using a jig-saw. Use the number 5 drill bit to make two holes through the backboard into the brackets; and also through the shelf down into the brackets. Spread wood glue on all the joining edges, and then screw them together with wood-screws.

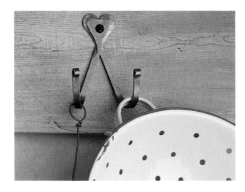

2

Apply one coat of shellac to the whole unit.

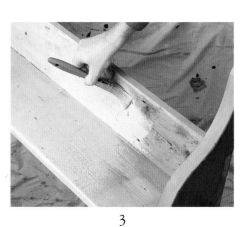

3

Use the 2.5 cm / 1 in brush to apply a coat of Dusky Blue emulsion.

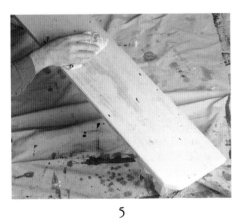

4

When dry, apply a coat of Aqua Spring.

5

Immediately afterwards, use a damp cloth to wipe the paint off in some areas.

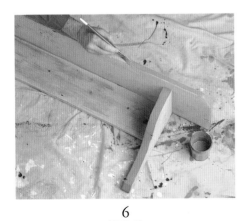

6

Paint the edges of the shelf and brackets with Precious Jade.

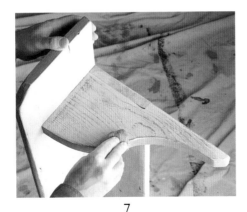

7

Rub away some of the dried paint using wire wool. This will reveal the wood grain along the edges.

8

Finally rub down with medium-grade sandpaper to smooth the finish and reveal the grain. Screw in the hooks. Attach to the wall by drilling through the backboard to make holes for long wood-screws. Use suitable wall fixings, if necessary.

Painted Dresser

*If there is one item of furniture that typifies country style in most people's minds,
it must surely be the dresser. A sturdy base cupboard topped with china-laden
shelves is an irresistible sight.*

This dresser was made by a local carpenter using reclaimed pine, but a dresser can easily be made up using a sturdy chest of drawers combined with a set of bookshelves. The trick is to make sure that the two are balanced visually, with the height and depth of the shelves suiting the width of the base. You can join the two unobtrusively by using strong steel brackets at the back, and painting will complete the illusion that the two were made for each other.

The washed-out paint finish is achieved by using no undercoat and rubbing the dried paint back to the wood with sandpaper and wire wool. Alternatively you can rub some areas of the wood with candle wax before you begin painting; the candle wax will resist the paint, leaving the wood bare.

MATERIALS

*dresser, or combination of shelves
and base cupboard
shellac
household paintbrushes
Crown Compatibles emulsion
paint in shades 'Dusky Blue',*

*'Quarry-tile Red' (optional) and
'Regency Cream'
household candle (optional)
medium-grade sandpaper and
wire wool
varnish in shade 'Antique Pine'*

1

Apply a coat of shellac to seal the bare wood.

2

Paint the dresser Dusky Blue, following the direction of the grain. Allow to dry.

3

If desired, rub candle wax along the edges of the dresser before painting with a second colour.

4

The wax will prevent the second colour from adhering completely, and will create a distressed effect. Add the second colour, if using.

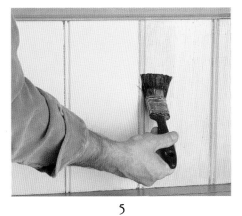

5

Paint the backing boards Regency Cream,
again following the direction of the grain.

6

When the paint has dried, use medium-
grade sandpaper and wire wool to rub back
to bare wood along the edges, to simulate
wear and tear.

7

Finally apply a coat of Antique Pine
varnish to the whole dresser to
protect the surface.

Details and Accessories

Little details complete the country interior – candle
sticks or sconces holding beeswax candles; shelves
decorated with lace, ribbon or punched leather;
brightly painted tins stocking the larder;
and baskets, copper pans, and dried flowers hung
from butcher's hooks, making a delightful display
in the kitchen. These ideas, and more, are all
simple to make and will transform your home.

Wooden Candlesticks

This pair of matching wooden candlesticks have been made from old balusters that were removed from a stair rail. This is an easy way to make something from turned wood without having to operate a lathe yourself. Balusters can be bought singly from wood merchants or DIY stores.

The only special equipment needed is a vice and a flat-head drill bit, to make a hole in the top of the baluster large enough to hold a candle.

The candlesticks have been painted in bright earthy colours, giving a matching pair fit to grace any country table.

MATERIALS

saw
2 wooden balusters (reclaimed or new)
2 square wood off-cuts
medium- and fine-grade sandpaper
wood glue
vice

electric drill fitted with a flat-head drill bit
acrylic paint in bright yellow, red and raw umber or burnt sienna
household and artist's brushes
clear matt acrylic varnish
soft clean cloth

1

Cut out the most interesting section of the baluster and a square base; this one measures 7.5 × 7.5 cm / 3 × 3 in. Roughen the bottom of the baluster with sandpaper.

2

Very slightly, chamfer the base with fine-grade sandpaper. Glue the two sections together with wood glue.

3

Hold the candlestick securely in the vice and drill a hole for the candle 2 cm / ¾ in in diameter and 2 cm / ¾ in deep.

4

Paint with two or three coats of bright yellow acrylic paint.

5

Apply a coat of orange acrylic paint (add a touch of red to the yellow acrylic).

6

Tint the varnish to a muddy brown, by adding a squeeze of raw umber or burnt sienna. Brush this over the orange.

<u>7</u>

Use a crumpled cloth to lift some varnish and
reveal the colour below.

CAUTION

When using wooden candlesticks do not
leave burning candles unattended or allow
the candle to burn right down, as the wood
may catch fire.

Woollen Patchwork Throw

Believe it or not, this stunning chair throw cost next to nothing to make, and was finished in an afternoon! It is made from pure woollen scarves and remnant wool fabric. The scarves come from charity shops, and can be bought for pennies. You will be spoilt for choice, so choose a colour scheme derived from your remnant. The throw is lined with a length of old brocade curtain, but a flannel sheet would also be suitable, especially if you dyed it a dark colour.

The only skill you need for this project is the ability to sew a straight line on a sewing machine: and tartan scarves provide good guidelines to follow. Clear a good space on the floor and lay the fabric and scarves out, moving them around until you are happy with the colour combinations. Cut out the first central square. The diamond shape will need to be hemmed and tacked before you sew it to the centre of the first square; after this, each strip of scarf will just need to be pinned and sewn in position.

The throw could easily be adapted to make a bedcover, and, because of the fine-quality wool used for scarves, it will be exceptionally warm. The challenge with this throw is to resist draping yourself in it, instead of the chair!

MATERIALS

scissors
about 1 m / 1 yd wool fabric
selection of plaid and plain
woollen scarves
pins, thread and sewing machine
old curtain or flannel sheet,
for lining

1

Cut out a 46 × 46 cm / 18 × 18 in square of your 'background' fabric. Choose the pattern for your central diamond and cut a square, using the width of the scarf as the measurement for the sides. Turn the edges under 1 cm / ½ in and tack. Pin and sew the diamond in position.

2

Choose two scarves and cut them into four rectangles. Position them along the sides of the square, with the matching patterns facing each other. Sew them in place and trim off any excess.

3

Cut out four matching plain squares and pin and sew them into the corners. Check on the right side, to make sure that the corners meet accurately. Cut four strips of the background fabric to fit the sides.

4

Cut out four corner pieces of the scarf used for the central diamond, 14 cm × 14 cm / 5½ in × 5½ in. Sew a square to one end of each strip of background fabric.

5

Pin and then sew these long strips in position around the edge of the patchwork.

6

Cut a plain scarf into four strips lengthways and sew these around the outside edge, overlapping at the corners to complete the square.

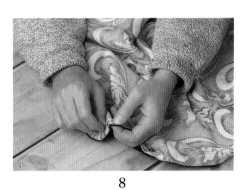

7

Cut the lining to fit and sew the two pieces together, with their right sides facing inwards.

8

Turn inside out and sew up the seam by hand. Press, using a damp cloth and dry iron.

Plaited 'Rag-rug' Tie-backs

Tie-backs are an attractive way of getting the maximum amount of daylight into the house. It is surprising how much difference a few inches more exposure of window panes can make to the light in a room, so unless your windows are huge, it is well worth tying your curtains back into the wall. This idea has a real hands-on feel and can be made to co-ordinate or contrast with existing curtains.

This method of plaiting scraps of fabric has been stolen from rag-rug makers, and if you have always wanted to make one, this may be just the introduction that you need! If you have any fabric left over from your curtains, you could incorporate this into the plaits. If not, one plain colour that appears in your curtaining will have a harmonizing effect on the whole scheme.

MATERIALS

*scraps of fabric cut into 7.5-cm /
3-in wide strips
safety pin
needle and thread
scissors
strip of fabric for backing (one for
each tie-back)
2 D-rings for each tie-back*

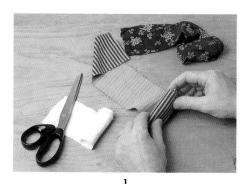

1

Roll up the fabric strips, leaving a workable length unfurled.

2

Join three strips together, rolling one fabric around the other two and pinning them together with the safety pin. Attach the ends to a chair or any suitable stationary object or anchor them under a heavy weight. Begin plaiting, rolling the strips into tubes as you go, so that the rough edges are turned in and concealed. Make tight plaits. The tie-back needs to be at least 50 cm / 20 in long and four plaits deep.

3

Work until you have the required length and number of plaits. Lay the plaits flat and sew the edges together using a large needle and strong thread pulled up tight. Keep the plaits flat when you turn at either end.

4

Cut a backing strip, allowing enough fabric to turn under 1.5 cm / ⅝ in all round. Attach the D-rings at either end as you slip-stitch the lining into place.

Lace and Gingham Shelf Trimming

The lacy look may not suit every room, but it can add a very French touch to a dresser or kitchen shelf. The contrast between stout enamel pans and fine cotton lace can be quite charming; in French country homes, crochet lace is pinned up for display on any shelf available.

There are so many different lace designs available, that the decision will have to be a personal one. You may go for an antique hand-crocheted piece or a simpler machine-made design. The pointed edging chosen here suits a china display very well.

There is something both cheerful and practical about gingham. It is perfectly suited to edging food-cupboard shelves, where the pattern is strong enough to stand out against all the different packaging designs. The combination with lace is fresh and pretty.

MATERIALS:

strips of lace the length of the cupboard shelves, plus extra for turnings
cold tea
small bowl

scissors
double-sided tape
gingham ribbon the length of the sides of the shelves
all-purpose glue

1

To tone down the brightness of this new lace, it was dipped into a bowl of cold tea. The stronger the brew, the darker the colour, so adjust it by adding water to lighten the dye, if necessary. Press the lace when dry and cut it to the correct length.

2

Apply the double-sided tape to the vertical sides of the shelves and peel off the backing tape. Cut the gingham ribbon to fit and seal the ends with a little glue, which will dry clear and prevent the ends from fraying.

3

Stick the gingham ribbon to the verticals, carefully smoothing it out and keeping it straight. Start at one end, and keep the ribbon taut.

4

Apply double-sided tape to the edges of the shelves, overlapping the gingham.

5

Seal one end of the lace with a small amount of glue. Stretch it along the tape, cut it to fit and seal the edge. Repeat for the other shelves.

French Bread Bin

*The kitchen and meal-times play a central role in country life, entailing warm
winter suppers when the nights have drawn in, or long, languorous lunches
in the height of summer. Crusty bread is an integral part of any meal, and
this stylish bread bin will bring a touch of French country style to your kitchen.
The same design could be used in a hallway or by the back door
to hold umbrellas or walking sticks.*

The pattern provided in the template
section could be given to a carpenter, or,
if woodworking is a hobby, made at
home. The stand has been made from
reclaimed pine floorboards, which are
quite heavy and give it stability, as does
the moulding used to broaden the base.

The decoration is called ferning and was
very popular in Victorian times. Dried or
imitation ferns (florist's sell fake plastic
or silk ones) are sprayed with aerosol
mounting adhesive and arranged on the
surface, which is then spray-painted. It
dries very quickly and the ferns can then
be lifted off. The effect is stunning and
very easy to achieve.

MATERIALS

wood for the stand (see pattern)
tracing paper or transfer paper
jig-saw or coping saw
wood glue and 2.5 cm / 1 in
panel pins
hammer

For the decoration
shellac
household paintbrush
newspaper
masking tape
spray adhesive
selection of artificial ferns
spray-paint in black, dark green
or dark blue
fine-grade sandpaper
clear matt varnish

1

Apply two coats of shellac to seal and colour
the bare wood.

TO MAKE THE STAND

Cut the timber to the dimensions shown
on the pattern in the template section.
Mitre the edges. Trace the
pattern for the back detail and cut it out
using a jig-saw or coping saw.
Apply wood glue to all joining edges,
join them and then use panel pins
to secure them.

2

Working on one side at a time, mask off the
surrounding area with newspaper and masking
tape. Apply mounting spray to one side
of the ferns and arrange them on the surface.

3

Spray on the colour, using light, even sprays,
and building up the colour gradually.
Lift the ferns when the paint is dry.

<u>4</u>

Work on all the sides and the inside back panel in the same way.

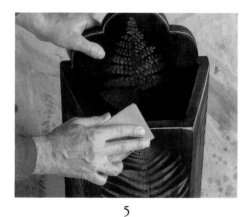

<u>5</u>

Sand the edges to simulate a time-worn look.

<u>6</u>

Finally, apply two coats of varnish to protect the fernwork.

Rabbit Dummy Board

A free-standing oversized rabbit will certainly provide both a focal and a talking point! Dummy boards originated as shop or inn signs; in the days when few people could read, a painted sign would indicate the trade being practised on the premises. The signs would either hang above the doorway or stand on a wooden block. You can give this rabbit a support to make it stand up, or hang it on the wall.

This project employs a mixture of old and new, as it is an original nineteenth-century engraving enlarged on a photocopier. The fine lines of the original thicken up with enlargement, but not enough to lose the effect of an engraving.

This project is great fun and fairly simple, and the only real skill required is that of cutting the shape out with a jig-saw. Personal experience has shown us that there are people who delight in this; so if you don't have a jig-saw — find someone who does!

MATERIALS

*wallpaper paste and brush
A2 (59.5 × 42 cm /
23¾ × 16¾ in) sheet of marine
plywood (or similar)
jig-saw
fine-grade sandpaper
shellac
household paintbrushes
varnish in shade 'Antique Pine'
clear matt varnish
scrap of wood for stand
PVA glue*

1

Photocopy the rabbit pattern from the template section, enlarging it to the edges of an A4 sheet. Cut the enlargement in half to give two A5 sheets.

2

Enlarge both of these up to A3 size. Depending on the machine, this process can be done in one step, or might take several enlargements.

3

Apply a coat of wallpaper paste to the plywood. This seals the surface and provides a key for the pasted paper.

4

Trim the 'joining' edges of the photocopies right up to the print, so that they can butt up against each other with no overlap. Apply a thin layer of wallpaper paste right up to the edges and stick the two halves together on the board. Smooth out any bubbles with a soft cloth and leave it to dry overnight.

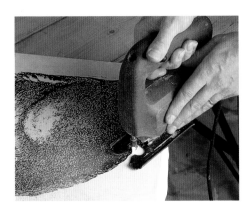

5

Use a jig-saw to cut out the shape, leaving a flat base. Using a jig-saw is not difficult, but you will need to practise to get the feel of it. Take your time.

6

Sand the edges of the rabbit smooth.

7

Seal the surface with a coat of shellac, which will give it a yellowish glow. Apply a coat of Antique Pine varnish, followed by several coats of clear varnish.

8

Trace the pattern from the template section. Use it to cut out the stand. Rub down the edges with fine sandpaper and glue in place

Curtain-pole Hanging Display

The Victorian clothes airer made use of the warmth above the range in the days before tumble driers. These days they are seldom used for their original purpose; instead they are adorned with hooks that hold copper pans, baskets and other delights.

However, not all ceilings are suitable for a heavy airer, and some are not high enough for a hanging display of this sort. For the country look without the creaking timbers and bumped heads, try this attractive, painted curtain pole.

The wooden curtain poles used here can be bought from any DIY store.

MATERIALS

curtain pole, plus turned finials (not brackets)
2 large 'eye' bolts for ceiling beam
medium-grade sandpaper
emulsion paint in green, red and cream
household paintbrushes
clear varnish tinted with raw umber acrylic paint
2 equal lengths of chain
cup hooks and butcher's hooks for displays

1

Using the pole as a measuring guide, position and screw into the ceiling or beam the two 'eye' bolts. These must be very sturdy and firmly fixed. Sand down the pole and finials, and then paint the finials green.

2

Paint the pole red. When the pole is dry, paint the cream stripes 6 cm / 2½ in from the ends.

3

Sand the paint in places to give an aged look. Fit the finials on the ends of the pole. Apply a coat of tinted varnish. Attach the lengths of chain to the 'eye' bolts. Screw in two cup hooks to the pole in the correct position to line up with the bolts. Attach the butcher's hooks for hanging your decorations, hang up the pole and add your display.

Embroidered Pelmet

In France, pelmets such as this one are often pinned up above windows
that do not need curtains, but that would otherwise be too plain.

The embroidery is simply made from a few basic stitches and is quite suitable for a beginner to attempt. Gingham curtains provide a simple contrast without detracting from the embroidered pattern, but you could make calico curtains and embroider them with the same designs – if you have time and have fallen under the embroidery spell!

MATERIALS

tracing paper
dressmaker's transfer paper or carbon pencil
1 m / 1 yd calico, cut into 2 strips 20 cm / 8 in deep
needle and embroidery thread in 4 colours
scissors
curtain wire

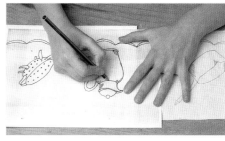

1

Enlarge the patterns from the template section to approximately 10 cm / 4 in. Use transfer paper or carbon pencil to transfer the patterns on to the calico.

2

Depending on your knowledge and level of skill, embroider each of the designs. A simple chain-stitch can be used, but cross-stitch, stem-stitch, back-stitch and French knots will add variety.

3

Use satin-stitch to make the scalloped edge. Carefully trim the edge. Sew a seam along the top edge and thread a length of curtain wire through it. Gather to fit the window.

Leafy Pictures

Delicate skeletonized leaves come in such breathtakingly exquisite forms that
they deserve to be shown off. Mount them on hand-made papers and frame them
to make simple yet stunning natural collages.

MATERIALS

wooden picture frame
sandpaper
paint
paintbrush
backing paper
pencil
scissors
skeletonized leaf
picture framer's wax gilt
hot glue gun and glue sticks
mounting paper

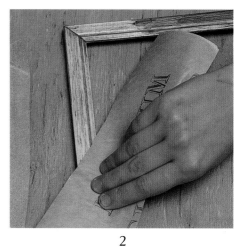

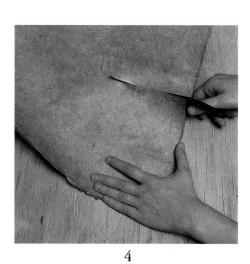

1

Take the frame apart and sand it down to
provide a key before painting. A translucent
colourwash has been used for painting here,
but any paint will do.

2

Allow the paint to dry, then sand the
paint back so you're left with a wooden frame
with shading in the mouldings, plus a
veil of colour on the surface.

3

Use the hardboard back of the frame as a
template for the backing paper. Draw around
it with a pencil to form a cutting line.

4

Cut the backing paper out.

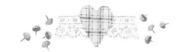

<u>5</u>

Prepare the leaf by rubbing with picture
framer's wax gilt. This does take a little time
as the gilt has to be well worked in.

<u>6</u>

Stick the backing paper on the frame back,
glue the mounting paper in the centre and
attach the leaf on to that. Here, the leaf is
centred with the stalk breaking the edge of
the mounting paper. Finally, put the
frame back together.

Provençal Herb Hanging

*Fix bunches of fresh herbs to a thick plaited rope, add tiny terracotta pots to give
the design structure and then fill it in with garlic and colourful chillies to
make a spicy, herbal gift full of Provençal flavour, for anyone who loves to cook.*

MATERIALS

*hank of seagrass string
scissors
garden string
florist's wire
fresh sage
fresh thyme
fresh oregano
2 small flowerpots
6 florist's stub wires
2 garlic heads
hot glue gun and glue sticks (optional)
large dried red chillies*

1

Cut six lengths of seagrass string about three
times as long as the desired finished length of
the hanging. Take two lengths, fold them in
half and place them under a length of garden
string. Pass the cut ends over the string and
through the loop of the fold, thereby
knotting the seagrass on to the garden string.
Repeat twice with the remaining four
seagrass lengths. Divide the seagrass into
three bundles of four lengths and plait them
to form the base of the herb hanging.

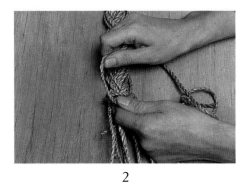

2

Finish the end of the plait by binding it with
a separate piece of seagrass string.

3

Using florist's wire, bind the herbs into small
bundles and tie each one with garden string.
Use this to tie them to the plaited base.

4

Wire the flowerpots by passing two stub
wires through the central hole and twisting
the ends together.

5

Wire the pots to the base by passing a stub
wire through the wires on the pots, passing
it through the plait, and then twisting the
ends together.

6

Tie garden string around the garlic heads
and tie these to the base. Wire or glue
the chillies into position, and fill the pots
with more chillies.

Shell Candle Centrepiece

An old flowerpot, scallop shells gleaned from the fishmonger or kitchen and smaller shells picked up from the beach make up a fabulous, Venus-inspired table-centrepiece. Either put a candle in the centre, as here, or fill it with dried fruits or flowers.

MATERIALS

hot glue gun and glue sticks
8 curved scallop shells
flowerpot, 18 cm / 7 in tall
bag of cockle shells
4 flat scallop shells
newspaper, florist's foam or other packing material
saucer
candle
raffia

1

Generously apply hot glue to the inside lower edge of a large curved scallop shell. Hold it in place on the rim of the pot for a few seconds until it is firmly stuck. Continue sticking shells to the top of the pot, arranging them so they overlap slightly, until the whole of the rim has been covered.

2

In the same way, glue a cockle shell where two scallops join. Continue all around the pot.

3

Place another row of cockles at the joins of the first row. Glue flat scallop shells face upwards to the bottom of the pot, first at the front, then at the back, and then the two sides, to ensure the pot stands straight.

4

Fill the pot with packing material and place a saucer on top of this. Stand a candle on the saucer.

5

Tie raffia around the pot where it joins the stand.

6

Decorate the stand with a few more cockles, if you like. Stand a few more curved scallop shells inside the original row to create a fuller, more petalled shape.

Spice Topiary

*Fashion a delightfully aromatic, culinary topiary from cloves and star anise,
pot it in terracotta decorated with cinnamon sticks and top with a
cinnamon-stick cross. Sticking all the cloves into the florist's foam is both
easy to do and wonderfully therapeutic.*

MATERIALS

*small 'long Tom'
flowerpot
knife
cinnamon sticks
hot glue gun and glue sticks
florist's dry foam cone,
about 23 cm / 9 in tall
small florist's dry foam cone
florist's stub wires
large pack of star anise
cloves*

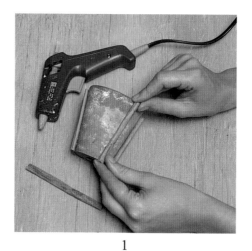

1

Prepare the pot by cutting the cinnamon
sticks to the length of the pot and gluing
them in position.

2

Trim the top of the larger cone. Cut the
smaller cone to fit inside the pot. Put four
stub-wires upright in the pot so they project
above the foam.

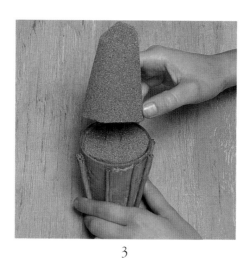

3

Use the stub-wires to stake the trimmed cone
on top of the foam-filled pot.

4

Sort out all the complete star anise from the
pack, plus any that are almost complete —
you'll need about 20 in all. Wire these up by
passing a wire over the front in one direction,
and another wire over the front in another
direction to make a cross of wires. Twist the
wires together at the back and trim
to about 1 cm / ½ in.

_5_

Start by arranging the star anise in rows down the cone – about three each side to quarter the cone. Put two vertically between each line. Next, just fill the whole remaining area of cone with cloves, packing them tightly so none of the foam shows through.

_6_

Glue two short pieces of cinnamon stick into a cross. Wire this up, and use it to decorate the top.

Natural Christmas Decorations

Raid the store-cupboard and scrap box, add garden clippings plus dried fruit slices, and you have the ingredients for delightful Christmas decorations that can be individually hung or tied on to the tree, or strung on to twine to make a garland.

MATERIALS

florist's stub wires
bundles of twigs
picture framer's wax gilt
dried bay leaves
dried pear slices
fabric scraps
dried apple slices
dried orange slices
small elastic bands
cinnamon sticks
gold twine
beeswax candle ends

1

Wire together bundles of twigs, and then gild them by rubbing in picture framer's wax gilt.

2

Make up the fruit bundles. Make a small loop at one end of a florist's stub wire. Thread on some dried bay leaves, and then a dried pear, passing the wire through the rind at the top and bottom. Make a hook at the top.

3

Tie a scrap of coloured fabric to the bottom loop and a scrap of green (synthetic chiffon is shown) at the top, to look like leaves. Make the apple-slice bundles by threading on first the thick apple slices, and then the bay leaves.

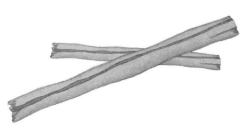

4

Wire up pairs of thinner-sliced apples by passing a wire through the centre and twisting the wires together at the top. Wire up the orange slices in the same way.

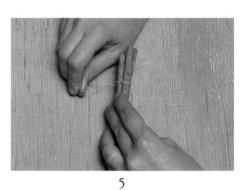

5

Use small elastic bands to make up bundles of cinnamon sticks.

6

Either hang each decoration directly on the tree or make up a garland to hang on the tree or at the window. Here, they have been strung together using gold twine. The beeswax candle-ends are simply knotted in at intervals.

Everlasting Christmas Tree

This delightful little tree, made from dyed, preserved oak leaves and decorated with tiny gilded cones, would make an enchanting Christmas decoration. Make several and then group them to make a centrepiece, or place one at each setting.

MATERIALS

knife
bunch of dyed, dried oak leaves
florist's wire
small fir cones
picture framer's wax gilt
flowerpot, 18 cm / 7 in tall
small florist's dry foam cone
4 florist's stub wires
florist's dry foam cone,
about 18 cm / 7 in tall

1

Cut the leaves off the branches and trim the stalks. Wire up bunches of about four leaves, making some bunches with small leaves, some with medium-sized leaves and others with large leaves. Sort the bunches into piles.

3

Prepare the pot by cutting the smaller foam cone to fit the pot, adding stub-wire stakes and positioning the larger cone on to this. Attach the leaves to the cone, starting at the top with the bunches of small leaves, and working down through the medium and large leaves to make a realistic shape. Add the gilded cones to finish.

2

Insert wires into the bottom end of each fir cone and twist the ends together. Gild each cone by rubbing on wax gilt.

Fruity Tree

Glycerined leaves make a perfect foundation for any dried topiary. You can buy them in branches, ready glycerined for use, or glycerine your own garden prunings. Here, they have been wired into bunches for a fabulous, full look.

MATERIALS

secateurs
3 branches of glycerined
beech leaves
florist's stub wires
dried pear slices
florist's dry foam ball, about
13 cm / 5 in diameter
flowerpot, 18 cm / 7 in tall

1

Cut the leaves off the branches and trim the stalks short. Wire up small bunches of four or six beech leaves and twist the ends of the wires together.

2

Pass a stub wire through the top of each pear slice and twist the ends together.

3

Completely cover the portion of the ball that will show above the pot with beech leaves.

4

Add the pear slices and put the ball into the pot.

Trompe-l'oeil Dhurrie

Canvas Floor Cloth

Stencilled Border

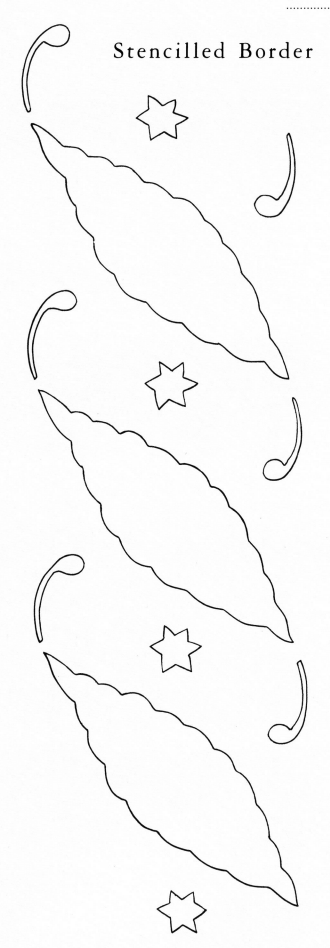

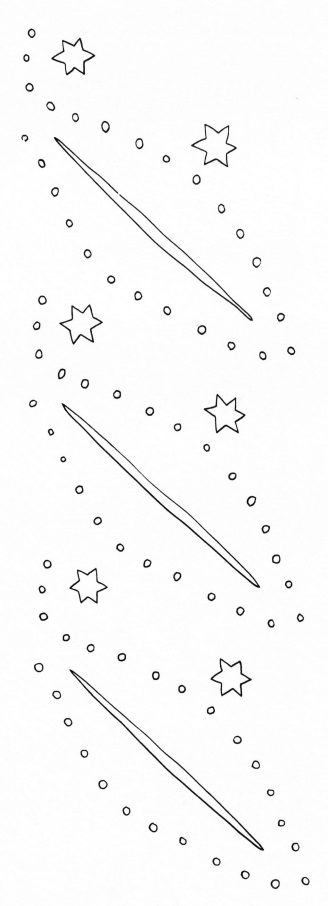

Foam-block Painting

Acorn and
Oak-leaf Border

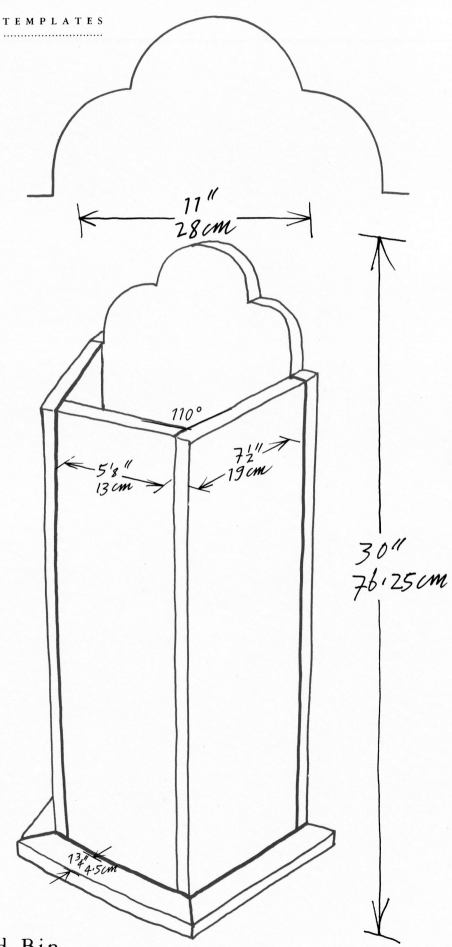

French Bread Bin

Painted Chest

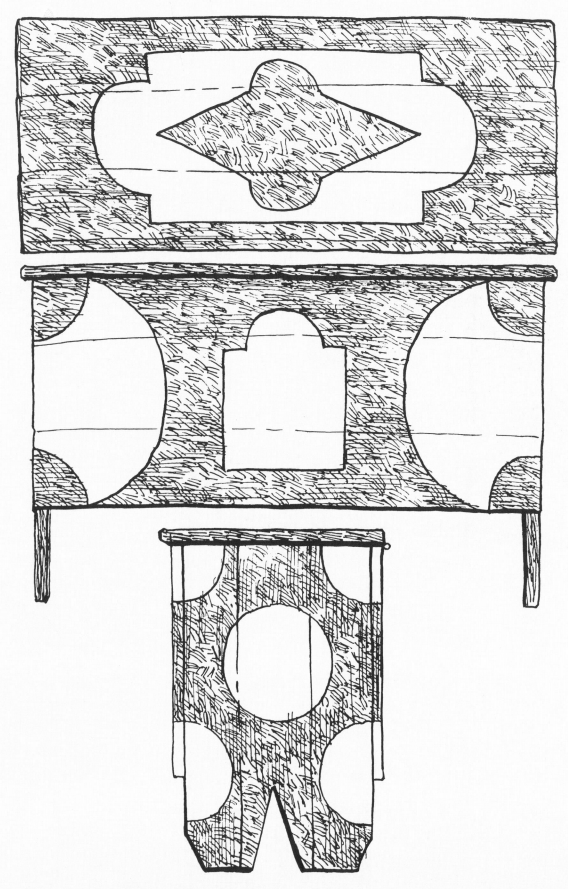

Rabbit Dummy Board

Shelf Bracket and Dummy Board Stand

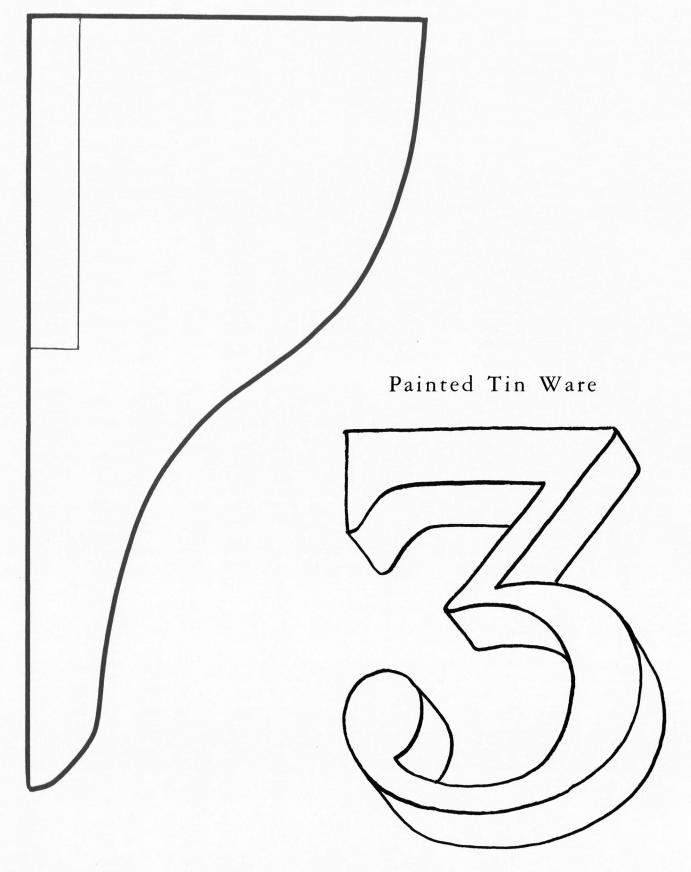

Painted Tin Ware

Embroidered Pelmet

Index

Suppliers

Appalachia The Folk Art Shop,
14a George Street,
St Albans, Herts AL3 4ER;
Tel: 01727 836796; Fax: 01992 467560

Brats,
281 King's Road,
London SW3 5EW;
Tel: 0171-351 7674;
also 624c Fulham Road,
London SW6 5RS;
Tel: 0171-731 6915
(Suppliers of Mediterranen palette paints)

Farrow & Ball Ltd,
Madens Trading Estate,
Wimborne, Dorset BH21 7NL;
Tel: 01202 876141; Fax: 01202 873793
(Suppliers of National Trust paints)

Hill Farm Herbs,
Park Walk, Brigstock,
Northants NN14 3HH;
Tel: 01536 373694; Fax: 01536 373246
(potted fresh herbs, dried herbs and flowers,
dried flower decorations).

Manic Botanic,
34 Juer Street,
London SW11 4RF;
Tel: 0171-978 4505
(made-to-order floral decorations).

Paint Magic,
116 Sheen Road,
Richmond,
Surrey TW9 1UR;
Tel: 0181-940 5503; Fax: 0181-332 7503
(Suppliers of paints and varnishes)

Shaker Ltd,
25 Harcourt Street,
London W1H 1DT;
also 322 King's Road,
London SW3 5UH.
Mail order to Harcourt Street address
or by telephone on 0171-742 7672

Somerset Country,
779 Fulham Road,
London SW6;
Tel: 0171-371 0436

Robert Young Antiques,
68 Battersea Bridge Road,
London SW11 3AG;
Tel: 0171-228 7847